NORWEGIAN
TAPESTRIES

Looking at
APPLIED ART IN NORWAY
A series of books dealing with applied art, past and present.
Editor: Cand.mag. Johanne Huitfeldt

Aase Bay Sjøvold

NORWEGIAN TAPESTRIES

*Translated from the Norwegian
by Elizabeth Seeberg*

C. HUITFELDT FORLAG A/S
OSLO

First published in Norwegian 1976
by C. Huitfeldt Forlag A/S, Oslo

ISBN 82-7003-031-7

Printed in Norway

Typeset and printed by Napers Boktrykkeri, Kragerø, and
bound by Emil Moestue A/S, Oslo.

Frontispiece: Detail from a Norwegian 17th-century tapestry.
This Renaissance courtier on his fiery steed is woven in vivid,
harmonizing colours. The black and white outlines of the
figures emphasize the strict composition (see fig. 1).
Museum of Applied Art, Oslo.

Cover photo by Atelier Teigen, Oslo.

Contents

The Baldishol Tapestry

A spectacular find

Fig. 1. The motifs of this beautiful tapestry are difficult to interpret. Perhaps we have illustrations for the legend of "Guimar the knight". 17th century, 195 x 130 cm (see frontispiece and p. 52).
Museum of Applied Art, Oslo.

The 17th-century church at Baldishol in Hedmark was demolished in 1879, and all its contents were sold by auction.

In 1886–7 Louise Kildal was living near this church, at Hoel, the farm of her brother-in-law. One day she went to the farm Baldishol, together with some other people, to see if there was anything left after the auction. On 12th August 1907, the following interview with her appeared in the newspaper Morgenbladet: "First they brought me some old paintings from the church. I was not very interested in these. Then came some of the turzets, but they were not really suitable for a private home. I asked if they had any tapestries or other textiles. They did, an antependium and an old rag. And that old rag was – the Baldishol tapestry! It was full of clay, and it was almost impossible to see what it actually consisted of. After the church had been demolished, it had been thrown into a cubby-hole, and it would probably have been eaten by moths if it had not been saved in time. In the church it had been lying under the sexton's footstool, because there was such a draught from the cracked, old floor. Surely no other sexton, past or present, has ever had such a priceless rug at his feet!"

Louise Kildal often told her family about the

thorough cleaning of the tapestry, so that the pictures and patterns again became distinct, and the colours surprisingly pure and clear. She repaired the piece to the best of her ability, and hung it up in her Kristiania home. This is where H. A. Grosch, the director of the Kristiania Museum of Applied Art first saw the tapestry, which his museum then acquired (see colour plate).

In his book about the Baldishol tapestry (1918), Hans Dedekam tried to date it, and to relate it to its proper environment. His exhaustive stylistic analysis employs comparative material from many countries, and he concludes that the Baldishol tapestry may have

Fig. 2. The Baldishol tapestry, detail illustrating the month of April: a man holding a flower in his raised hand stands beside a tree with birds. H: 120 cm.
Museum of Applied Art, Oslo.

been woven in Norway, but no earlier than 1180–90. Today it is generally held that it cannot be older than from the first half of the 13th century – it may even be somewhat later.

What we know as the Baldishol tapestry today is no more than a fragment of a longer frieze. Its height, 118 cm, is intact – this was the width of the fabric when it was still in the loom. Both ends have been cut or torn off, and the fabric between these raw edges is 203 cm long. The material is wool from the *spelsau*, the Scandinavian short-tailed sheep, and the warp threads are surprisingly coarse as compared to the thin weft threads. This gives the tapestry a full, deep texture. The white areas are woven with a linen weft. Vegetable dyes were used for the wool, which still appears in clear red, yellow, green, dark blue, and several shades of a lighter blue. Dedekam proposed the theory that the blue dye used was woad. This plant was in use in Norway at an early date, probably being grown for officinal use as well as a dye. The earliest find of the fruit of the woad comes from the Oseberg burial (c.850). The pigments of this tapestry have not as yet been analysed, so that our knowledge about them is purely hypothetical. The colours have faded surprisingly little, and their decorative intention is still apparent.

Pictures of the months

This tapestry has two panels with human figures, separated by a pillar. The panels are crowned by arches rising from the pillar; at the bottom of the tapestry runs a frieze with palmettes, at the top, a narrower border with a stylized wave pattern.

In the left panel we see a man standing beside a flowering tree with three birds, fig. 2. In his raised right hand he holds a palmette-like flower, and a fourth bird appears on that side. He is wearing a long-sleeved, split tunic reaching down to his ankles. His feet reach down into the palmette border, the top of his bearded head and the flower into the clumsily inscribed arch. The letters PR and ILI can be deciphered; together with a curlicue, perhaps an inverted S, they provide a clue to the motif: this is the month of April.

The right panel has a horseman in full armour, with a ringed byrnie, a conical helmet with nose-guard, and a dragon-shaped shield, fig. 3. His spurred foot rests in a stirrup. The lance in his right hand is lowered, his left lifts the horse's reins. The helmet of this determined young warrior goes over the inscribed arch at the top; the distorted letters here are damaged. The reading May has been suggested, as a logical sequel to April, but in their preserved form the letters defy all interpretation, although the horseman may well represent the month of May. This would agree with southern and western European medieval pictures of the months, although the horseman is usually depicted with a falcon there, and is thus less belligerent than our armed warrior.

If the Baldishol tapestry, which is so thick, once had twelve panels, one for each month, it would have been

The Baldishol tapestry, birds from the month of April.

Fig. 3. The Baldishol tapestry, detail with the horseman on his dappled red horse against a pale blue background. H: 120 cm.
Museum of Applied Art, Oslo.

more than 12 m long, a length difficult to wind on the beam of the loom. It is also possible that several pieces hung side by side, perhaps they were sewn together, or perhaps the series was never complete.

The Baldishol tapestry is unique among Norwegian medieval material. We have no other tapestry here, woven in this technique at so early a date.

The Oseberg tapestries, which are frequently referred to in connection with the Baldishol tapestry, are woven in an entirely different technique; their iconography is different, and they form part of quite another tradition.

The sources and the weaver's problems

Even abroad we have little material for comparison. The literary sources are not very clear, and the preserved 12th and 13th-century tapestries woven in this technique can be counted on the fingers of one hand. They were all woven in the German region, where Cologne and Lower Saxony had achieved a high standard of textile art at an early date. Quedlinburg, southeast of Hanover, was an important centre during the early Middle Ages. Patronized by princes, weaving flourished in the castles and convents there. The cathedral of Halberstadt, near Quedlinburg, still has two long tapestry friezes, as well as tapestry fragments, all woven locally between 1150 and 1200. The earliest of these shows St.Michael and the dragon, together

Fig. 4. The Archangel Michael killing the dragon. Detail from a longer tapestry illustrating the story of Abraham. The colours are green, dark blue, reddish brown, pale yellow and white, with dark and white outlines. Probably woven ca. 1150. Cathedral of Halberstadt, E. Germany.

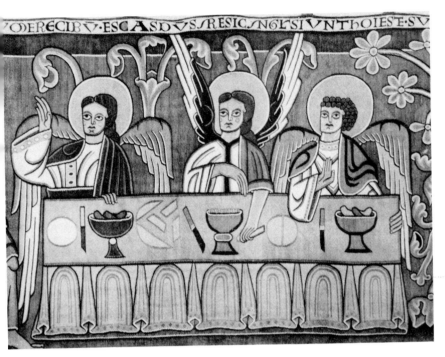

Fig. 5. Detail of a tapestry illustrating the story of Abraham: the three angels at Abraham's table. Probably woven c. 1150 (see fig. 4). Cathedral of Halberstadt, E. Germany.

with scenes from the life of Abraham; it may throw light on our Baldishol tapestry, figs. 4, 5.

The two parts of the Halberstadt frieze shown here illustrate the German weavers' skill and precision in transposing the cartoons from which they must have worked. The tip of a wing, a flower, the edge of a garment, a foot and the dragon's tail with foliate finials break the frame of the panel – these are intentional effects adding to the dynamic rhythm of the composition. The inscription is clear and easily read, and all the details combine to form an organic whole.

The weaver who made the Baldishol tapestry was confronted with the same problems, but did not master them entirely. It was obviously difficult to fit the figures in with the rest of the composition. The inscriptions are jumbled and distorted, many of the lines and shapes are imprecise, and we note especially that the ornamental background of the figures is so incoherent as to be almost meaningless. But even so this tapestry is fas-

13

cinating, admirable by virtue of the weaver's skill in reproducing the motifs so vividly, with such intense expression. But this is not a case of "artistic licence" – this is the work of a professional craftsman, but we have reason to believe that the tapestry was produced under more primitive conditions than those obtaining at the textile centres of the day.

At these textile centres there was close contact between the artist responsible for the design and the sketches, the master who prepared full-scale cartoons, and the weavers who executed the design, and thus one could there achieve results unattainable for smaller, peripheral workshops. They had to resort to simplified methods: not only must the weavers have had a number of designs to work from, or they found their inspiration in manuscript illuminations, in paintings and stained glass, in wood-carving and decorative metalwork, all according to the wishes of the client. The skill of those who prepared cartoons from such originals may have varied greatly.

Thus the final product depended not only on the weaver's skill and his conception of his model, but also on the original to be copied and the quality of the cartoon. Our two representations of months may originally have been created by an artist conversant with the late Romanesque style, but some time must have passed between the creation of the original designs and that of the tapestry, as the subdued style and the distortion of parts of the motifs show.

Cultural contacts

The original may well have been created abroad – the closest points of contact with regard to style and motif are then to be found in northern France and in England! Our horseman has been compared to William the Conqueror's advancing warriors as they appear on the more than 70 m long embroidered tapestry from Bayeux, fig. 6. This must have been embroidered during the period from 1070 to 1090, to commemorate the Norman conquest of England in 1066. Even though the

Fig. 6. Detail from the Bayeux tapestry, "the Battle of Hastings", 1066, with English foot-soldiers fighting a Norman horseman. Embroidered with several colours of wool on coarse linen. Probably made between 1070 and 1090. H: 70 cm. Musée de la reine Mathilde, Bayeux, France.

difference in time is considerable, the close Norwegian contact with this part of western Europe may indicate the origin of Baldishol – like so much of 12th and 13th-century Norwegian art, it may have sprung from the stylistic traditions of this region.

English stylistic impulses occur on the stave church portal from Hylestad in Setesdal – on the basis of coins found here, this church can probably be dated to the reign of Håkon Håkonsson, i.e. before 1263, fig. 7. The carved portal illustrates the legend of Sigurd Favnes-bane from the Volsunga Saga, and includes details reminiscent of the Baldishol tapestry, such as the undulating tree trunk, the birds, Sigurd's split tunic and the harness of his horse, fig. 8. The Baldishol tapestry

15

and this portal must owe their inspiration to the same cultural sphere.

The Baldishol tapestry may have been woven in

Fig. 7. Portal from Hylestad stave church, Aust-Agder. Motifs from the Volsunga Saga. 13th century.
University Museum of National Antiquities, Oslo.

Fig. 8. Detail from the left jamb of the Hylestad portal. Sigurd Favnesbane and Regin the dwarf are roasting the dragon's heart under a tree, the birds are warning Sigurd against Regin. At the top Sigurd's horse, Grane, carrying Favne's treasure.
University Museum of National Antiquities, Oslo.

16

France or England for a Norwegian client, or it may possibly have been woven in Norway, but there is no evidence suggesting that tapestry weaving became so common in medieval Norway as to create a tradition. Such textiles were presumably hung in some churches and at court, in environments which were in close contact with the more central parts of Europe during the high Middle Ages.

European Background

Spread and development

It seems that the European decorative textiles of the kind which we here term "tapestries" had their origins in Persia and in the Near East during the last millenium BC. The art must have developed in Christian Europe from the Carolingian period onwards, by way of Coptic, Islamic and, not least, Byzantine weavers. The dearth of preserved textiles and literary sources makes it impossible to trace this development in any detail.

Originally this technique was used for decorative details on garments, draperies and hangings, woven in silk or thin, fine wool on a linen warp. From the 11th century onwards, a gradual development must have taken place in central parts of Europe. In time, Byzantine functions and forms were abandoned, techniques and tools were adapted to European materials, requirements and style. Certain elements of the Halberstadt tapestries suggest a connection with early phases of this development, while technical details of the Baldishol tapestry show a closer connection with the mode later adopted by more provincial European tapestry workshops.

Tapestries woven in this technique were probably taken into use in western European churches and castles in the course of the 12th century. We know that Paris had several tapestry workshops in the 14th century, and that the two main types of tapestry loom were known in medieval France: "basse-lisse", with a horizontal warp, and "haute-lisse", with a vertical warp. The material used was wool, but later the warp was most often of linen, while the finest tapestries also included threads of silk and metal. Many of the weavers must have been itinerant craftsmen, working for the churches and castles requiring their services. These medieval tapestries were hung on the bare stone walls of the castles, in the choirs of the great cathedrals. They

Fig. 9. Detail from the Apocalypse series of tapestries, with motifs from the Book of Revelations. "The woman in scarlet" on the beast with seven heads and ten horns. Woven in Nicolas Bataille workshop, Paris, between 1375 and 1380. Musée d'Angers, France.

Fig. 10. Calendar leaf, January, with the signs of Sagitarius and Aries. The Duke of Berry sitting at a banqueting table. On the rear wall a large, French tapestry with battle scenes. From "Très Riches Heures du Duc de Berry", beginning of the 15th century. Musée Condé à Chantilly, France.

were often woven in several pieces, from cartoons drawn by artists.

The famous "Apocalypse series" in the cathedral of Angers, woven between 1375 and 1380, fig. 9, are the earliest French tapestries still preserved. From later periods we have more, their number increasing as the centuries pass. This applies to the long friezes, which are much used in the Middle Ages, as well as to the upright ones, more common in later periods. The finest period of medieval tapestries coincides with the great days of the Dukes of Burgundy, during the 15th century, fig. 10. These beautiful tapestries represented an investment to which immense prestige attached, and thousands were woven in the districts near Paris and in northern France. Their motifs are in keeping with the current development in painting – in fact they are paintings executed in textile. During the 16th century they were even equipped with naturalistic "wooden" frames, woven like the rest.

At that time France no longer held the leading position. Now there were tapestry workshops all over Europe, and Flanders, including Brabant and Brussels, was by far the most important region, fig. 11. There tapestries inspired by Flemish and Italian painting were produced. In 1661 Louis XIV of France made a successful effort at re-establishing French tapestry weaving: in Paris a large workshop was installed in a house formerly occupied by the family Gobelin, a family of dyers. This institution, which still exists under the name "Manufacture Nationale des Gobelins", was primarily intended to produce tapestries for the palaces of France, and "gobelin" still means "tapestry" in several languages.

ig. 11. Detail of the
order of a tapestry with
enus illustrating one of
ne months. Brussels, ca.
650. The borders forming
ne frame of tapestries
woven in Flanders were
ndependent compositions.
ienna, Kunsthistorisches
Museum.

Tapestries for the burghers

Tapestry weaving was an exclusive art, a specialized craft. Influential clients, able to lead production into the channels they desired, were responsible for the growth of this art in Europe. The centres of production were mostly in districts where wool of a suitable quality

19

was locally available, for large amounts of wool were required. But during the 15th century, smaller workshops were founded in some districts, producing tapestries for churches and monasteries, for the gentry and the emerging wealthy middle classes.

The convent workshops produced antependia and other church textiles. The cathedral of Bamberg has a 15th-century antependium, which shows the Virgin and Child, together with the three magi and saints. The workshop's symbol appears at the lower edge of the Virgin's cloak: a small nun with her tapestry loom, fig. 12. The Crucifixion, with the Virgin Mary and St.John, forms the central motif of another antependium, presumably woven in the Netherlands, fig. 13. Antependia woven in this technique were still in use in Norway after the Reformation, as we shall see below.

Long friezes were also woven in this technique, especially in southern Germany and Switzerland. Their subjects are more popular, frequently alluding to fables or to worldly love and marriage. These friezes were very popular among the gentry and the burghers far into the 16th century, hung up on festive occasions.

But this new, growing clientele demanded more than pictorial wall hangings woven in this technique – they also wanted tapestry covers for chair backs and the

Fig. 13. An antependium from the end of the 15th century. German region. Golgatha, where the Cro is raised, is covered in flowers; medieval buildings in the background. An art dealer's in Munich, 1975

20

ig. 12. The little nun
itting at her tapestry loom
as placed herself and her
vorkshop under the
rotection of the Virgin
Mary. Detail from a
apestry antependium in
ne cathedral of Bamberg.
1: c. 10 cm. End of 15th
entury.

seats of chairs and benches. Table runners, bedspreads and bed hangings were also produced. When upholstered furniture became fashionable during the 17th century, many workshops, large and small, specialized in tapestry-woven furnishing fabrics, fig. 14.

Technically these new objects are closely related to the true tapestries, but their choice of motifs is far more complex. Only a few of them are inspired by contemporary figurative lithographs, prints and paintings; the majority are based on common European sources, whose main components are foliate and heraldic motifs, and which also include a highly varied assortment of ornaments which might be used to form repeats

Fig. 14. Renaissance chair. Back and seat covered with tapestry woven covers showing motifs from the life of Christ. Back: entry into Jerusalem within a wreath of flowers, the four evangelists in the corners. 17th century. Hamburg? The chair is from north-western Norway.

covering a ground, fig. 15. Below we shall try to relate the Norwegian tapestries from the post-reformatory period to a wider context of development, and there this wealth of material can be included only in as far as it throws light on the actual pictorial tapestries.

We have a great deal of information about craftsmen who left the great centres of weaving in northern France and Flanders during the troubled years at the end of the 15th and the beginning of the 16th century, with their unstable political and religious conditions. These men then settled in Holland and northern Germany. Some weavers were summoned by German princes, who no longer wished to be dépendant on the great Flemish workshops, and royal tapestry workshops were established in Denmark and Sweden, but none of these efforts resulted in lasting traditions. Other weavers found a market for their products in the cities of northern Germany, such as Hamburg, Wismar, Lüneburg, Lübeck and Rostock.

During the first half of the 16th century a bourgeois school of tapestry weaving grew up near the southern border of Scandinavia. Here small pictorial tapestries were produced, as well as cushion covers and other decorative tapestry fabrics. We know that this work also included women, not only as the employees of some workshop, but also as self-employed tapestry

Fig. 15. This pattern, a variation of the palmette motifs of Renaissance silks, occurs on several tapestry cushion covers. The example shown is from a bedspread. The palmettes are alternately blue and red, with green and yellow crosses on a brown ground, and white and brown outlines. 167 × 140 cm.
Museum of Applied Art, Oslo.

Part of the border of "The wisdom of Solomon", fig. 18, probably woven in Norway at the time when Johanne Jensdatter lived in the Skien district.

weavers; others wove at home, to cover their own requirements.

Flemish weaving and witches

Legal documents tell us that Anne Pedersdotter, the widow of the well-known Bergen clergyman Absalon Pedersen Beyer, was burnt at the stake in 1590. During her tragic trial it appeared that she had been angry with Giert the joiner and his wife, because they had not let her have a "frame" for weaving "Flemish". This frame had been intended for Anne's daughter Suzanna. Thus we know that "Flemish" weaving was practised by this Bergen clergyman's family during the years just before 1600. The word "Flemish" refers to Flanders, the unchallenged centre of tapestry weaving at that time. Textiles produced in this technique were known as *flamsk* (Flemish) in Norway, a term still in use in Sweden today. The Flemish loom – upright, and with two beams – must have been introduced into Norway by weavers from abroad. The weaver sat while working, and wove from the bottom up. Even though it was a novelty in Norway, this loom was well known in the rest of Europe, and there must have been several types and sizes.

Yet another witch was burnt in Bergen, in 1594, the tapestry weaver Johanne Jensdatter. We know that she owned a house in the city, and that she taught young girls weaving. She had come to Bergen from Skien on the Oslo Fjord, in the county of Telemark, where she had also worked as a tapestry weaver. She is the only Norwegian "Flemish" weaver whose name – and fate – we know; she is of especial interest since it seems that the district of Skien was one of the first centres of "Flemish" weaving in Norway.

During the latter half of the 16th century Renaissance tapestries had come as a new fashion to Norway, and in all likelihood provincial weavers from northern Germany and Slesvig came to this country and practised their craft here. The first weavers may have included men as well as women, but in the course of time this craft was practised exclusively by women in

23

Norway. Professional weavers worked to order, and they must surely have trained young girls, as Johanne Jensdatter did. Some of these girls in turn became professional tapestry weavers, but there were also some upper-class women who wove only for their own, private use. More women learned this art in the course of the years, but it always remained the prerogative of the few. We must again note that this "Flemish" weaving, which became so popular in Norway during the 16th century, does not in any way seem to be related to native, medieval tradition. On the contrary – it represents the farthest flung echo of the development which had taken place in Europe during the 15th and 16th centuries.

We do not know where and when the first generation of "Flemish" weavers settled in Norway – both Skien and Bergen are attested, but we cannot disregard the hypothetical possibility of the Trondheim district either. The sea was the highway joining Norway to the countries of the North Sea, but the road from Denmark led through Scania and Båhuslen to Østfold. We see a somewhat similar development in Sweden, where professional weavers started to produce tapestries for the middle classes and the landed gentry during the 17th century. The end of the 18th and the beginning of the 19th century saw a revival of tapestry weaving in Sweden, in the form of Scanian folk art.

Two imported tapestries

Some pictorial tapestries were imported into Norway, not only before they were produced in this country, but also during the time when tapestry weavers were active here. The preserved textiles show that most of this import came from small workshops in Holland or northern Germany. A great deal must have come from Hamburg, and it is not unlikely that agents in that city effected the sale of fabrics from workshops in the surrounding districts. One of these tapestries, which probably came to Norway as soon as it was finished, around the year 1600, may serve to illustrate the

Fig. 16. The elegant woman dressed in Renaissance fashion may be Helen of Troy, the two "Roman warriors" Prince Paris and his companion abducting her. The composition, where the central panel is surrounded by a wide, rectangular frame with fruit and flowers, is typical of Renaissance tapestries. About 1600 or somewhat earlier. 236 x 174 cm. Museum of Applied Art, Oslo.

Vine with clustes of grapes and branch with legumineous fruit. Detail of border, see fig. 16.

24

development of the northern European Renaissance style in the smaller workshops on the periphery of the Flemish region, which were nevertheless under the direct influence of that centre of production, fig 16.

The weaver must have worked from a precise, well-composed cartoon. There are three figures in a landscape, framed by a richly ornamented, somewhat stylized wide border with fruit and flowers. The figures are in motion, the resulting foreshortening was apparently not easy for the weaver. The figures overlap, and this produces an effect of depth, accentuated by the light and shade in the draperies, which is achieved by means of "hachures" (see p. 86). The effect of distance in the landscape is enhanced by the contrast between the tree and other vegetation in front, and the houses behind.

This tapestry is woven in fairly coarse wool on a linen warp; although it is faded there is still much more colour than is normal for Norwegian tapestries. Here we have one of the many classical subjects popular during the Renaissance. The motif may be the rape of the Sabine women or – perhaps more likely – Paris with his companion, abducting Helen of Troy. Classical motifs were little used by Norwegian tapestry weavers – this is a foreign element, which may serve as a contrast to set off our own tapestries, woven in this country.

Fig. 17. The aristocratic gentleman on his death-bed, safeguarded by Christian virtues and biblical texts surrounding him. On the far left, a woman who is probably his wife, to whose order this "memorial tablet" was woven. Probably Rostock, 1560s–1570s. 164 x 215 cm.
Museum of Applied Art, Oslo.

The aristocratic gentleman of the Leksvik tapestry, see fig. 17.

Another tapestry, said to have hung in Leksvik church in Nord-Trøndelag, probably serving as a memorial tablet, is shown on fig. 17. The shape is unusual – it looks as though the bottom had been off, so that only the upper part of a larger tapestry remains. There are fringes on all four sides. Figurative tapestries are always woven in such a way that the figures lie on their sides while the fabric is on the loom, and thus the sides of the tapestry represent the starting and finishing edges of the fabric. But our tapestry has selvedges at the top and bottom, which means that it was never higher than it is today, and the multicoloured fringed border may well be original. Thus this tapestry is a good example showing how independently a weaver could interpret his patterns and their compositions, perhaps according to the wishes of his customer.

The subject is the death-bed of an aristocratic gentleman. With him are four women, who symbolize the Christian virtues: CONSTANCY, LOVE, HOPE AND FAITH. A female figure standing in a niche on the left probably represents the man's widow, who had ordered the tapestry. The function of the six women in the upper niches is less clear. The Bible verses all over the tapestry closely recall Kristiern Pedersen's New Testament of 1529, and therefore some think that this piece was made in Norway. However it is more likely to have been made in N. Germany, the region which has yielded the closest parallels, several tapestries resembling that from Leksvik. We cannot simply assume that a minor Norwegian workshop exported tapestries to N. Germany at this early date: the university in Rostock had many Norwegian students during the 16th century, and there was close contact between Rostock and urban Norway. In any case – this memorial tapestry was woven by a highly skilled professional weaver, as its exquisite quality shows. The materials include wool, linen, silk and metallic thread to highlight the small, colourful details. The elegant garments in German fashion, correct in materials as well as in cut, indicate that the cartoon must have been designed during the 1560s or 1570s.

In tapestry weaving the weft was beaten in with a comb beater. This one was probably used by a professional tapestry weaver. The upper part of the handle is wooden. Marked with the date 1668. From Lier, Buskerud.
Norwegian Folk Museum, Oslo.

Tapestry Weaving in Telemark

The Song of Solomon

Telemark, especially the district of Skien, was of importance during the latter half of the 16th century, for at that time the region experienced a period of rapid economic growth. There are good natural harbours, and with the advent of the gate saw, the timber trade flourished. This must be the main reason for tapestry weaving gaining ground here at an early date; our small group of Telemark tapestries dates from the period 1575–1600.

Most important, perhaps, is a specimen from Hjartdal, fig. 18. The motif has long been known as "The

Fig. 18. From the Song of Solomon. King Solomon and his bride, together with courtiers, seated in an enclosed garden (hortus conclusus), protected from evil spirits. Probably from the 1570s. 244 x 186 cm. Found in Hjartdal, Telemark.
The Nordiska Museet, Stockholm.

Court in the Garden". A crowned king sits on the left side of an apple-tree, together with two courtiers – on the right, a woman wearing a richly embellished gown has her ladies-in-waiting with her. The king and the lady hold doves, there is a peacock on the gate, and small dogs or "foxes" run about in the foreground. A town is seen in the background at the top of the picture, and the motif is surrounded by a twining floral border. Today the colours are blue, yellow and brown, with traces of green. Most of the red picks have changed colour, leading to an entirely different general impression. The figures are more frontal, more rigid than those of the two preceding Renaissance tapestries, and the "hachures" give the effect of an allover pattern. Like most Norwegian tapestries, this has a woollen weft on a linen warp.

This motif has recently been re-interpreted – it represents, in fact, a condensed version of the Song of Solomon. The king is Solomon, the lady Sulamit, his bride-elect. Thus this must be a bridal tapestry, its motif being interpreted literally as well as symbolically.

All biblical subjects connected with weddings and fertility were popular tapestry motifs. There are north German Renaissance tapestries with Esther and Ahasuerus, Solomon and the Queen of Sheba, David and Bathsheba, and the story of Lot and his daughters. These motifs also occur in Scandinavia, and thus it is not easy to decide whether late 16th-century tapestries found in Norway were imported, or whether they were woven in Norway by an immigrant craftsman. We have this problem with two tapestries illustrating the story of Lot, both of them said to come from Heddal.

Lot and his daughters

The first of these tapestries has a clearly defined picture panel, with a wide and luxuriant, although somewhat diffuse, border with fruit and flowers, fig. 19. Iris, apples and grapes can be seen among the foliage. Within the panel Lot, wearing a crown, is seated under an appletree, and there are small houses in the distance. His daughters are pouring his wine, but neither jug nor cup are shown.

It seems clear that the cartoon must have covered a larger motif than that included in the panel. The main elements of the composition recall those of the Paris and Helen tapestry. Although the conventional "hachures" of the Lot tapestry tend to have av confus-

Fig. 19. Lot and his daughters, a popular motif of tapestries woven for the urban middle classes. This type of composition is, like fig. 16, based on Flemish Renaissance tapestries. Faded. From Heddal, Telemark. Embroidered mark: DM 1575. 261.5 x 163.5 cm.
Norwegian Folk Museum, Oslo.

ing effect, certain details of the garments show that the original may date back to the middle of the 16th century. Another tapestry based on the same design is preserved – it was woven in Denmark or northern Germany at the beginning of the 17th century. Embroidered on our Lot tapestry we find D M 1575 and a simple owner's mark, and it is not unlikely that the tapestry was woven in Norway at that date.

The next Lot tapestry follows a different model, and thus a different cartoon. There are two scenes: the

Fig. 20. Two episodes from the story of Lot: at the bottom, the flight from the burning cities, at the top, Lot's daughters pour his wine during their sojourn the mountains. 230 x 208 cm. Lüneburg or Wismar 1579.
Norwegian Folk Museum Oslo.

narrow, lower panel shows Lot and his daughters flee-
ing from the burning cities, while Lot's wife remains
alone, as a pillar of salt, in the desolate landscape, fig.
20. In the upper panel Lot's daughters are again pouring his wine, and here the cup and the flasks of love
potion are shown. A border with small "sentries" on
brackets, carrying palm leaves, pelicans, masks, cartouches and flowers frames the tapestry on three sides.

The figures, garments and draperies are more natural
here, the movement freer. Again the original may be
rather earlier than the tapestry. Above Lot's hat we see
his name and a coat-of-arms with SMEMD 1579; the
owner's mark is the same as above. This tapestry is said
to be the work of a girl who had been abroad, and it is
thought to have been at the farm Sem in Heddal ever
since. Such a tradition is not the same as proven fact,
but it is by no means unlikely that particularly capable
women should have been sent abroad in order to learn
the art of tapestry weaving when this had become
popular in Norway.

From the style and the general appearance of this tapestry we may infer that it is closely related to others from Lüneburg and Wismar, where two pictures were often combined into one tapestry. At the present stage it seems most likely that our tapestry is of north German origin. In fact it has no more in common with the other Heddal tapestry than the subject. The owner's mark and the initials may indicate a closer connection; it is clear, however, that these tapestries are the work of two weavers.

The professional weavers who came to Norway must have had cartoons, patterns and sketches with them, and as a rule they also had access to copperplate engravings of popular motifs by well-known artists. These were enlarged into cartoons and colours were added. In Germany cartoons are known to have been divided into narrow strips. Our intinerant weavers may also have had patterns of various motifs, borders and texts, which would enable them to combine designs from different sources, often according to the wishes of the customer. They are not likely to have copied their models slavishly in Norway – they recreated them instead. Below we shall see the effect of this practice during the first half of the 17th century.

The gift of the magistrate

Mats Mørkholt was magistrate of Sandsvær and Lardal from 1615 until 1625, when he moved from the district. He and his wife, Anne Persdatter, may have given the tapestry known as the "Sandsvær antependium" to a local church. All we really know about the history of this tapestry is that the Museum of Applied Art purchased it in Numedal in 1887, fig. 22.

The central motif of the Sandsvær antependium, as of the above 15th-century specimen (see p. 20), is the Crucifixion. Here, too, the cross is raised on a flowering meadow, and we see "Jerusalem" in the background. On either side of Christ are the coats-of-arms of the presumed donors, who may be seen on the extreme left. Next comes a group of three people

Fig. 22. Mats Mørkholt and his wife had this so-called "Sandsvær antependium" woven, probably around 1625. Once brightly coloured, now very faded. 122 x 223 cm. Museum of Applied Art, Oslo.

35

standing in front of a towering tree with one flowering and one bare branch growing out of the trunk. Beside the cross stands St. John the Baptist, with a halo, pointing up towards Christ. The other two figures have often been taken to represent Abraham and Isaac, but the seated, naked figure may well be Man, on whom the grace of God has been bestowed by way of baptism,

Fig. 23. Frontispiece of Christian III's Bible, with scenes from the Old Testament and the New Testament. Copperplate engraving, printed in 1550, and based on an engraving by Lucas Cranach the elder.

while the standing figure may represent the Old Testament and the Law – perhaps this is Moses.

On the right of the Crucifixion we see the Resurrection of Christ. Death and Satan lie vanquished under His feet, two awestruck soldiers are watching the miracle. On the far right we have Eve with her fig leaf, holding an apple. There was no room for Adam, but

Fig. 25. Detail from the "Sandsvær antependium" Christ crucified is depicted with greater realism than the other figures.

the serpent appears as a kind of picture puzzle among the foliage.

Many of the details would seem to show that this antependium was inspired by several different sources, among them the title page of Christian III's Bible, which appeared in Copenhagen in 1550, fig. 23. This is, in turn, based on an engraving by Lucas Cranach. Uddevalla Museum in Båhuslen has a tapestry which may derive from the same title page. It is said to have hung in the museum – once a manor farm – since the 18th century, fig. 24. It is interesting to note how the artist and the weaver intepreted and adapted the original motif in the cartoon and in the finished product. The similarity between these two does not, however, permit us to infer that the Sandsvær specimen is modelled on that from Uddevalla.

On the Sandsvær tapestry the figure of Christ is obviously larger and more realistic than the other figures, fig. 25. The others are rigid and frontal, and the weaver mastered neither the foreshortening nor the twisting of the bodies. The buildings in the background are crowded together, their towers all awry. The figures are highly stylized, the drapery schematic, and the patterns are reduced to geometric figures.

These changes are not, as has previously been held, a result of the influence of an earlier Norwegian tradition in popular art. On the contrary – the motifs were handed on from one weaver to another, sketches and cartoons were redrawn and changed as they wore out. New details were added, others were taken away. In the course of this development, which spread farther and farther from the original centre of production, the original models were simplified. A process of stylization took place, connected forms were broken up, the effect of depth disappeared. The figures, now frontal, grew rigid, the details lost their significance, and figurative representation became decorative ornamentation.

Detail from the "Sandsvær antependium", showing "Jerusalem", the city in the background, see fig. 22.

GERT FRØNNICK: IAHANNE:
LAURITSDAATERANNO1630

OHERREGVDEFTERDITGODE
TSNE OMVENDALOMNVLOKE
OCIDOVACIORFREMMEIEG
VILORALDRIGFORGLEMME

Bread, wine and the water of life

The Last Supper is the subject of a tapestry from
Søndeled church near Risør, fig. 26. Christ and the
apostles are seated in a room with brick walls, and
small, leaded lozenge windows. Christ is sitting under a
baldachin, and the apostles are grouped around the
table so that eight are sitting on the same side as Our
Lord, there is one at either end of the table. The two
whose backs are turned on the spectator turn their faces
to the right, so that they appear in profile. And thus a
greater effect of space, of movement, is achieved than
in the Sandsvær antependium, while perspective is pro-

Fig. 26. "The Last Supper", woven for Gert Frønnick and Johanne Lauritzdatter in 1633. The cartoon, vividly realistic, had a wealth of detail, but the more sketchy part on the right must have been woven according to the weaver's own design. The tapestry is faded, and thus the fastest colour, pink, has become very conspicuous. Søndeled church, Aust-Agder.

vided by the buildings on the left. The weaver must have had a first-class cartoon, but the part on the right must have been added to make up the length, for the details here are sketchy, and one part has been restored with painted cloth.

The Søndeled tapestry is another example of a fabric with a border on three sides, with twisted ribbons connecting large flowers, pears and bunches of grapes. The jackets of the apostles are buttoned in front, and their narrow collars are edged with lace, details still in fashion when the tapestry was woven. Their large cloaks, however, are a more picturesque element, fig. 27. An inscription reads: GERT FRØNNICK

41

Fig. 27. Detail from "The Last Supper", showing an apostle.
Søndeled church, Aust-Agder.

IAHANNE LAVRITZDAATER ANNO 1630. Was this a gift from Johanne Lauritzdatter Marstrand to the church, in memory of her husband, Gert Frønnick from Tønsberg? Another inscription on this tapestry would seem to suggest this possibility.

When the old main building of the farm Sannes in Drangedal was torn down in 1823, a tapestry was found between two sets of panelling, fig. 28. The motif is again a biblical meal, the wedding at Cana. The crowned bride sits between the groom and the Virgin who, in turn, is talking to Jesus. Three courtiers are sitting opposite them, their backs towards the spectator. On the right, Jesus is watching while the wine

Fig. 28. Tapestry showing the wedding in Cana. Found under panelling on the farm Sannes in Drangedal. This tapestry once had many shades of red, but on the surface these have faded into a yellowish white. 160 x 185 cm. Museum of Applied Art, Oslo.

jugs are being filled with water. The musician, shown higher up than the wedding party, is probably standing on a balcony. Two fashionably dressed gentlemen, below left, are apparently commenting on the quality of the wine. Perhaps we should connect them with the inscription, which appears in reverse: *In Cana and Galilee Jesus turned water into wine Oluf Toresen 1653 D N D.* The frame, which consists of eight-petalled roses within a stylized zig-zag scroll, is one of the most common Norwegian tapestry borders. The fact that the inscription appears in reverse poses a problem: was this tapestry copied some years later from an original tapestry dating from 1653, or can there be some other reason? We shall not attempt a solution here. It is of interest to note that Olav Stiansson Sannes, farmer and county sherrif, bought Drangedal church with its land

43

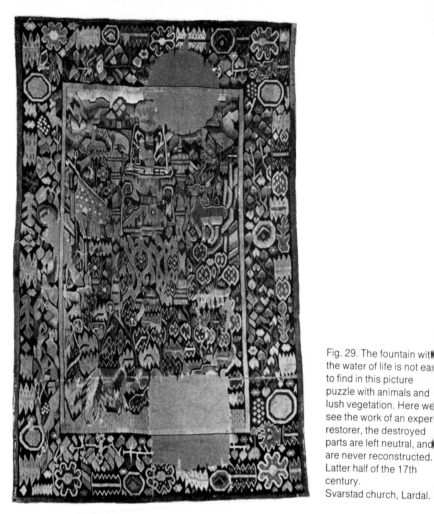

Fig. 29. The fountain with the water of life is not eas to find in this picture puzzle with animals and lush vegetation. Here we see the work of an exper restorer, the destroyed parts are left neutral, and are never reconstructed. Latter half of the 17th century.
Svarstad church, Lardal.

in 1734. Perhaps the tapestry once hung in that church? Or was Oluf Toresen a Sannes?

One of the most popular of all Renaissance motifs is water running crystal clear from sparkling fountains, fig. 29. The idea of water as a symbol of life and rejuvination is ancient. Svarstad church in Lardal has a tapestry with a fountain between columns in a paradisean landscape; deer, hares, birds and small animals are peacefully grazing side by side. The central motif is framed by a wide floral border. This tapestry, surely originally based on a Flemish original, has degenerated into a kind of picture puzzle, whose details become apparent as one studies it. Two large pieces were at some time cut out of it, but in spite of this vandalism, a painstaking process of preservation has recreated the composition as the weaver conceived it during the latter half of the 17th century.

All the above tapestries must surely have been woven by professional weavers. They were hung in churches, or in upper-class homes. Well-to-do women who learned tapestry weaving probably concentrated on cushion covers and the like, which could be woven on a smaller high-warp loom. The tapestries we have studied so far are the work of professionals – they represent the Renaissance culture of the Norwegian upper classes, and this culture came to Norway partly by way of Skien.

Tapestries from one workshop may have found their way to many places. Professional weavers moved, they wove for new customers, and thus the knowledge of tapestry weaving was spread abroad. Upper-class women who had acquired this new skill might move with their husbands, and thus tapestry weaving was introduced into new districts. The wives of clergymen were an important medium in this cultural process. During the 17th century – especially the latter half – tapestry weaving spread from the towns to the country-side. In about 1700, when tapestry weaving was no longer at the height of fashion in the cities, a rural tradition was established, but the details of this process are not yet known. Especially many tapestries were taken into use in Gudbrandsdalen, but we do not know whether all the tapestries in use in this valley were actually woven here.

Fig. 30. The parrot was the favourite bird of Renaissance art. Detail from a tapestry cushion cover. Bergen? 17th century.
Bu, Hardanger.

Tapestry weaving never became common among the women of the farm – it remained an exclusive craft which few were in a position to practise. Nor were tapestries in general use throughout the country – they were first and foremost popular in the countryside of eastern Norway, fig. 30.

Fig. 32. Detail from "The
Feast of Herod", fig. 31.
c. 70 cm.

Bridal Tapestries

The Feast of Herod

Fig. 31. "The Feast of
Herod" is the subject of
this tapestry from Sjåk. In
the upper panel a woven
inscription: TORØ
RASMVSDAATER 1613.
Note the vivid, expressive
movements and the great
number of small details.
Somewhat faded. 218 x
150 cm.
Gudbrandsdalen?
Museum of Applied Art,
Oslo.

One of the most disputed of Norwegian tapestries, said
to come from Sjåk, is now in the Museum of Applied
Art in Oslo. It is the chef d'œvre of a group of 13
preserved tapestries with motifs from the feast of
Herod. In all of them the motif is divided into two
panels, separated by an inscription, fig. 31.

The lower panel shows Herod and Herodias, both
crowned, as the principal figures at a lavish banquet.
The hall has magnificent columns and leaded glass
windows, fig. 32. Below, on the floor, Salome is
sedately dancing with her partner, the music being
provided by a trumpeter. On the far left Salome,
standing under the leafy canopy of a big tree, accepts
St. John's head on a platter. All we see of the

47

excutioner is an arm and hand, offering her the platter, one leg, and the point of his sword. Our Lord is hovering in the cloud above this scene. The narrow upper panel has a horseman on the left, followed by a bearded man in a long cloak, wearing a ruff. He raises one hand in a meaningful gest, and holds an object, apparently a scroll, in the other. On his cloak we can read TORØ RASMVSDAATER 1613. Beside him stands a woman in a cloak and ruff, raising both hands, apparently in supplication. The identity of these two is uncertain. The scene on the right, framed by two columns, shows the Adoration of the magi. Heads (possibly angels) appear on the spandrels.

The inscription between the two panels can, with some difficulty, be deciphered: *St. John when his head was cut off for the dance of a whore anno 1 3?1.* At the top and the bottom the tapestry is finished with a zig-zag border with lattice work. Within the border, a motif of opposed lions is repeated seven times; at the top right the same motif shows a man between the two lions, fig. 33.

Fig. 33. Detail from the upper border of fig. 31. A man in an opening (portal?) flanked by wild beasts (lions?). H: 10 cm Museum of Applied Art, Oslo.

Fragment of tapestry with two pictures of months, found in Baldishol church, Nes, Hedemark. First half of 13th century or somewhat later. Museum of Applied Art, Oslo.

Tapestry. The three Magi and the Adoration, framed by an animal frieze. Skjåk, 1717. Museum of Applied Art, Oslo.

Tapestry, showing ''The Feast of Herod'', the three Magi and the Virgin with the Child. Gudbrandsdalen, 17th century. Museum of Applied Art, Oslo.

Tapestry, showing King Solomon and the Queen of Sheba. Latter half of the 17th century. W
the Museum of Applied Art, Oslo.

The life of St. John and the feast of Herod were motifs much in use in northern German and Scandinavian tapestries, and several versions occur. Our tapestry must surely be based on a source which included the executioner, possibly also the execution. The upper part may have been woven from a different cartoon, and added in 1613 for Torø Rasmusdatter. Who she was we do not know, but she was hardly the weaver. To the best of our knowledge weavers did not at that time sign their products with full name and date.

The Swedish scholar Ernst Fischer has subjected all the Herod tapestries to a detailed stylistic analysis. He assumes that ours is a copy of one woven for Torø Rasmusdatter in 1613. According to him, it may be the earliest of the group woven in Skjåk, and it must have been made by a skilled weaver shortly before the middle of the 17th century.

In a somewhat earlier study, Roar Hauglid maintained that the date 1613 was reliable. In an inspired article: "Omkring et billedteppe fra Skjåk", he concludes that "the Herod tapestry from 1613 is entirely unconnected with medieval Norway. It is, in all respects, an integral part of the Norwegian Renaissance, as we meet it among the upper classes. It was woven, not for a farmer's cupboard bed in Skjåk, but for a Renaissance bridal bed."

Neither of these scholars is able to provide irrefutable evidence for the preferred date. They agree that the roots of this tapestry are not to be found in peasant art, but that the motif later became popular in the upper parts of Gudbrandsdalen. It was modified each time it was woven, and with every new weaver. On this point the tapestries speak for themselves. See colour plate and figs. 34 and 35.

Few of these tapestries can be dated precisely, the dates woven into some do not always indicate the year they were made. The records of estates contain information to the effect that they were mainly used as bedspreads. The records for Aker 1656–70, for instance, have: *"1 Flemish bedspread woven in pictures"*. The word Flemish must refer to the technique.

Fig. 34. ''The Feast Herod''. The motif is reversed, the text illegible. Rigid, frontal figures, disintegrated background with decorative pattern fragments. On the tablecloth: BHD. From Romsdal? Museum of Applied Art, Bergen.

g. 35. The same motiv as fig. 34, ''The Feast f Herod'', even though the inscription refers to
ing Solomon's first judgement. ANO I AOD. A clear case of simplification; the figures in the
oper row probably belong to a different sphere of motifs. 194 x 140 cm. Museum of Applied
rt, Oslo.

Fig. 36. In the two top panels, Justice and Patience, with spread wings. Flower urns in the two lower panels. Quadrupeds and birds are hidden in the fabric. 192 × 148 cm. 17th century, Vågå.
Museum of Applied Art, Oslo.

Legendary figures and allegorical motifs

The biblical motifs used by tapestry weavers include some difficult to interpret today, perhaps also at the time they were woven. One of these tapestries, woven with a profound feeling for decorative effect, is most interesting: the rectangular central panel is divided into four, with a large, oval rosette with the head of a man with a ruff at the centre, see cover and fig. 1.

Ornamental friezes with the same opposed lions as on the first Herod tapestry run vertically and horizontally from the rosette. It has been suggested that the figures in the panels illustrate the Breton legend of

Guimar the knight who, while hunting, met a snowy white deer with a branch growing from its head. He was tempted to shoot the deer, but his arrow returned and injured him. The well-placed figure stands out clearly against a more chaotic background. A corded frame separates the motifs from the wide outer border, whose unusually large details are reminiscent of the oriental carpets popular on the Continent.

On the Leksvik epitaphium female figures personified the Christian virtues. A tapestry with the same arrangement of motifs as Guimar's legend has two winged female figures, fig. 36. The inscription tells us that they are the virtues of classical antiquity: IVSTISIA, left, has a monkey and a bird, while PATIINTIAE is flanked by two birds. The superfluous letters may be initials.

The two lower panels contain flower vases, birds and small animals. Flower vases were popular also for cushion covers woven in tapestry technique, fig. 37.

Fig. 37. Some of the tapestry motifs were also used on cushion covers. Flower vase with deer?, birds among the foliage. Colours today: red, yellow, orange, green and blue. 54 x 60 cm. Lom, Gudbrandsdal.

Fig. 38. The unicorn was a
fabulous beast with a long,
spiral horn growing from
the middle of its forehead.
Here we have two
unicorns standing guard
over a central motif,
possibly a coat-of-arms.
The implication is not
clear, especially as the
motif is highly distorted.
17th century. 213 x 140
cm.
Museum of Applied Art,
Oslo.

The wide border is simpler than that of the preceding tapestry, a zig-zag alternating with stepped triangles. Four tapestries woven from the same original are preserved, but they are by no means identical, and a comparison will show how the motifis disintegrated.

The tapestry shown on fig. 38 is unique. The central rosette dominates, and the head within it has become a small mask, surrounded by parallel rays. Thor B. Kielland called this motif "The Head of Medusa". This female monster of Greek mythology, fig. 39, with writhing serpents instead of hair, turned all who looked directly upon her to stone. But our ornament can also be interpreted in other, more obvious ways. Perhaps Christian symbolism may provide the solution. The rosette at the centre of the tapestry is placed like a coat-of-arms, even though the head is upside down in relation to the two guardians of the shield, the unicorns. In medieval Christian symbolism unicorns represent the pure, the innocent, the sacred aspect of the Virgin Mary, and they were an important motif, much employed by medieval art. Unicorns could be tamed by none except virgins, and the chase of the unicorn forms the subject of several late medieval tapestries.

Fig. 39. Medusa, as antiquity depicted her, 4th – 3rd century B.C. Sardonyx cameo, 4.5 cm. Museo Nazionale, Naples.

Fig. 40. Solomon proves his wisdom to the Queen of Sheba. Accompanied by ladies and a courtier, they are watching the children at play. Faded and defective. 1649. 225 x 165 cm. Svelvik, Hurum, Buskerud. Museum of Applied Art, Oslo.

The Wisdom of Solomon

The wise King Solomon has always appealed to the imagination, and his meeting with the Queen of Sheba, who put his wisdom to the test, reads like a fairytale. She asked Solomon which of two identically clad children was a girl, which a boy, and he solved the problem by noting how the children caught the apples he threw them.

This scene is depicted on northern German and on Scandinavian tapestries. It occurs on one woven in

ig. 41. The motif of "The Wisdom of Solomon" was oon distorted into figures wearing compact, patterned garments, their acial features quite chematic, see the small children's heads in the bottom row. The vivid, glowing reds have entirely disappeared from this apestry which once had strong, decorative colours. 7th century. 213 x 145 cm.
Museum of Applied Art, Oslo.

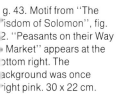

g. 42. "The Wisdom of
ºlomon", changed
most beyond
cognition. The children
ve disappeared, the all-
²er patterns dominate. A
mall supplementary motif
repeated in three
rsions (see fig. 43).
ded. Once strongly
ntrasting colours,
marily yellow and red.
ᵗh century. 193 x 134
n. Probably
udbrandsdal.
useum of Applied Art,
slo.

g. 43. Motif from "The
ʹisdom of Solomon", fig.
2. "Peasants on their Way
Market" appears at the
ottom right. The
ackground was once
ʹight pink. 30 x 22 cm.

Haderslev in Denmark in about 1550, and it may have
come to Norway by the end og the 16th century. A
tapestry with this motif, from Hurum in Buskerud, is
highly fragmentary, but fortunately the name and date
woven into the fabric are intact: KAREN PEDERS-
DATTER and 1649, fig. 40.

Solomon is seated on his baldachined throne, the
Queen of Sheba, crowned, stands beside him. Ladies-
in-waiting and a courtier attend them. The two children, with three playmates and two dogs, are shown at
the bottom. No trace of perspective remains, the
figures are frontal, and the ornamental effect is
enhanced at the cost of the composition. The patterned
garments, the background, and what remains of the
outer border have all been reduced to vegetal ornamentation.

The wisdom of Solomon is also shown on a group of six tapestries previously known as "The Court in the Garden". As so often happens, these tapestries came into the possession of different museums by way of agents, and thus their provenance is difficult to establish. Solomon, wearing his great crown and holding his sceptre, stands together with the Queen of Sheba and other figures. Only in a couple of cases are the children shown, and then merely as two small heads at the bottom, fig. 41. This central motif of all these tapestries must derive from the same model, perhaps from several copies of a copperplate engraving, or from enlarged sketches, which would explain the apparently rapid process of simplification and stylization, for the tapestries are not necessarily entirely contemporaneous. The latest of them may be that which, according to Trond Eklestuen, who had bought it, came from Vågå, fig. 42. Here the central motif and the border are both dominated by strictly two-dimensional all-over pattern; but for some reason unknown to us, the weaver introduced a small additional motif, fig. 43. This recurs three times, with varying details. It shows a farmer and his wife, dressed in their peasant clothes, carrying their produce to market. This motif is so naturalistic and so rich in detail that it is clear that the weaver had a good cartoon, although she felt free to make such small changes as the work might call for.

Another tapestry from the same group may or may not be as old as the date woven in – although back to front – indicates. It may date from 1620, or it may be a later copy. Initials and a name are also given: CAD KARIN and SA IFWER AS, fig. 44. The woman's name has the Swedish form – this is interesting in view of the fact that another tapestry of this group is said to come from Värmland in Sweden. National frontiers are not necessarily identical with cultural frontiers, and cultural impulses may travel either way. Solomon's wisdom can hardly have been the prerogative of one weaver only.

Fig. 44. This inscription appears reversed and upside-down in the border of a "The Wisdom of Solomon" tapestry. The names indicate cultural contacts with Sweden. Said to come from Trøndelag, Norway. Museum for Cultural History of Gothenburg, Sweden.

King Solomon and Christian IV

Pomp and circumstance attend the representation of
the first meeting of King Solomon and the Queen of
Sheba, which occurs on four tapestries, see colour
plate. The king, in his finest robes, complete with
sceptre and crown, meets his guest in the courtyard of
his palace. A distant city forms the background. The
queen approaches him, the symbol of her dignity, or
perhaps a gift, in her right hand, a plume in her left. A
lady-in-waiting and courtiers attend this meeting;
another man is watching the scene from the balcony.
The garments are in the fashion of the 1630s, and the

king, with moustaches and goatee, looks very much like Christian IV. In 1634 his son, the king elect, married Magdalene Sibylle. Is the courtier next to the king in fact the bridegroom, Prince Christian? Were there pictures of that wedding, pictures on which the cartoon from which these tapestries were woven, might have been based? Symbolism with hidden depths was popular at the time. The cartoon must have been made somewhat later than 1634, and the preserved tapestries do not include the first woven with this subject. All four of them must date from the latter half of the 17th century, and they form two pairs of closely related specimens. A distorted date on one of the most recent reads 1661. They all have inscriptions relating to this biblical meeting; one of them reads roughly: *Queen Nicola from the land of the Moors, to hear the wisdom of King Solomon.* This subject was surely woven for an upper-class clientele, who must have appreciated this subtle tribute to the popular king, see fig. p. 49.

Royal escutcheons quite often appear on tapestries. We have four Norwegian specimens with Christian IV's coat-of-arms, possibly executed on the initiative of the Court. The escutcheon is surrounded by cartouches, and in two cases it is framed by an animal frieze, fig. 45. The model is, as usual, highly distorted, but we can discern the leopards passants of Denmark. The thirteen coats-of-arms of the provinces and the inscription present a more difficult problem. The crown is of the open type, and the small angels flanking the top of the cross of Denmark are also shown.

Animal friezes were popular in Norwegian tapestry weaving; the present example includes a motley of living animals and supernatural beasts. Norwegian weavers must surely have continued to use Christian IV's coat-of-arms also after the king's death in 1648 – but when it was first employed, we do not know.

The three Magi

The symbolic significance of the tapestry motifs can no longer be ascertained. The representations certainly gave a great deal of scope to the imagination. The "Three Magi" tapestries are a good example of this. Theological interpretation had transformed the three wise men from the east, of whom the gospel according to St. Matthew tells, into three kings by the early

Fig. 46. The three Magi and the Adoration occupy the top of this tapestry. Below, King David stands in his balcony, and watches Bathsheba bathing in a fountain. Faded. 235 x 146 cm. Hol, Hallingdal. Norwegian Folk Museum, Oslo.

Middle Ages, and Norwegian medieval art represents them as crowned princes. European tradition calls them Caspar, Melchior and Balthasar; in this order they might represent old age (60), manhood (40) and youth (20). They might also stand for the three continents known to the Middle Ages, or they were shown as kings from Persia, Nubia and the legendary Sheba, in which case Balthasar was shown as a negro. They followed the star to Bethlehem, "and when they were come into the house, they saw the young child with Mary his mother, and fell down and worshipped him: and when they had opened their treasures, they presented unto him gifts; gold, and francincense, and myrrh."

Thor B. Kielland recorded 58 extant tapestries with the three magi – this must have been a popular motif. In some cases the three magi and the Adoration are combined with other motifs, as on Torø Rasmusdatter's tapestry, figs. 31, 46, 49. The majority of the three magi tapestries may, however, be divided into two groups.

The tapestries of the first group have four scenes in separate panels; in those of the second, the figural scenes appear within an oval frame. The four scenes of the first group are separated by a right-angled cross, a form typical of the Renaissance, fig. 47. The three Magi, mounted on their steeds, have one panel each. They are crowned and wear ruffs, short jackets and wide breeches. Balthasar is shown at the bottom right, for this king is beardless, while Melchior, beside him, can be identified by his short beard. Caspar, top left, has arrived at their destination. The kings are riding through a landscape with trees and low vegetation, and in the background we see a town below the starry sky. At the top right the two eldest kings kneel before Jesus, while the youngest stands a little way behind them. The Virgin is wearing a long, patterned gown and cloak. She has the headdress appropriate to married women, and the naked child sits on a linen cloth on her lap. Above the roofs and the stars we can discern a faded date, its letters somewhat distorted: ANNO 1625. The inscription on the horizontal arms of the cross is almost

Fig. 47. The three Magi and the Adoration in four panels. ANNO 1625 does not represent the ·ar of production. Faded, but traces of many different shades and colours, blue sky and red ·rth. 186 x 137. Said to come from Skjåk. Museum of Applied Art, Oslo.

illegible, but seems likely to read: *Hither (?) came the three kings who come from Sheba in the east.* The cross has narrow borders with geometrical patterns. On one of these tapestries groups of letters have been woven into the vertical arms of the cross; they may be the initials of the weaver and of the client. The outermost frame has a zig-zag with eight-petalled roses, very similar to other, painstakingly composed geometric borders with the same "roses" published in European pattern books, which were intended for use in various textile techniques.

The date 1625 appears on several tapestries of this group. It is never clear – in the end it disappeared. All these tapestries are based on the same composition, and it is quite evident that none of the preserved ones dates back to 1625. It seems most likely that a composition designed in 1625 was, after some decades had passed, copied and recopied. Our tapestries must date from the latter half of the 17th century, some possibly from its final years. The fact that the execution enables us to classify these tapestries into several sub-groups shows that they must be the work of several weavers, possibly working in different places.

Fig. 47b. Stars, known a eight-petalled roses in Norwegian folk art, in a barbed zig-zag, one of I most common tapestry borders.

The Magi framed by animals

In the next group an oval frame surrounds the Adoration and the kings, mounted on their steeds, fig. 48. In the corners between this frame and the outer border four heads of angels are placed diagonally. This is a Baroque form, and thus the original of this version must be later than the preceding. The figures appear on a neutral background, the space between them being filled with stylized plants and geometric patterns. It appears clearly from the faces, some in profile, others en face, that individuality and movement were important. The frame consists of two bands ending in spirals at the top and bottom; on them we see fabulous beasts as well as magpies, foxes, elephants and bears.

The two versions of the three Magi tapestries must be

Fig. 48. The three Magi within an oval frame with animals on a yellow ground. The backgroun of the oval panels is red Baroque composition. 1 x 144 cm. 1661? Skjåk? Museum of Applied Art, Oslo.

67

partly contemporaneous. The Baroque version remained in use longer than the other, as appears from certain dated tapestries which are somewhat different in character. They are more rigid and schematic, with frontal figures, see colour plate. There is also more open space between them. The oval frame has become octangular, the animal frieze includes a great number of real animals as well as fabulous beasts – even the heraldic lion of Norway is represented. Clearly the weaver picked her motifs at will. The initials on these tapestries may show that they were made for – perhaps by – one family. They all have dates, from 1684 to 1739. Eilert Sundt, the ethnologist, in 1863 mentions a tapestry from 1765, which he had seen at the farm Andvord in Bøverdalen.

The 18th-century tapestries form part of the popular art of upper Gudbrandsdalen. They were woven by local craftsmen or in the homes. Often it is difficult to distinguish between the work of a professional crafts-

Fig. 49. Lower part of a tapestry divided into two friezes. Here the magi a riding to the stable, to the Virgin and the Child. This tapestry has always bee predominantly blue. 17th century. W: 150 cm. Museum of Applied Art, Oslo.

man and that of a skilled amateur without examining the local milieu in detail; a meticulous analysis of all comparable textiles is also required. Most of the Norwegian tapestries are very faded, but some retain their clear colours. A couple of the most recent ones were so bright when they came to the museums that it seems as though they had lain in a dark chest even since they were woven during the first half of the 18th century. That dated 1717 has typically strong colours, with bright figures on a red ground. It also includes all the three borders which occur singly on the other three magi tapestries.

Several students of Norwegian tapestries have shown that there may be a connection between the Renaissance paintings found in churches and in profane buildings and some of the tapestry motifs. Such decorations were either painted straight on the wall, or on lengths of canvas, with swift strokes of the brush. They were bright and cheerful, but their colour spectre was limited. The figures were often drawn in dark outline before the details were added. Early sources make occasional mention of "painted hangings" in the possession of rich 17th-century farmers. This may refer to such canvas paintings, a phenomenon also known in other countries.

Fig. 49 b. Reconstruction drawing of a wall painting showing the three Magi and the Adoration. Hedsborg church, Telemark. 1604.

Three tapestries for three women

In 1761 a fine new dwelling-house was taken into use on the farm Glømsdal in Bøverdalen, the home of Rasmus Jonson Glømsdal and his wife Ingrid Gunnarsdatter. That same year their daughter Anna married Johannes Sivertsen from Vågå. Two elder daughters, Torø and Rønnaug, were already married. By pure chance three tapestries, which can be connected with the three Glømsdal daughters, are preserved. All bear the date

Fig. 50. Anna Rasmusdatter Glømdal' tapestry has God the Father, the generations Jesus, Anna's parents a Anna herself. This tapes is unique, with figures fu of colour contrasts on a deep blue ground, and a beautifully made fringe. 1760. 196 x 122 cm. Bøverdalen. Museum of Applied Art, Oslo.

1760. Two of them have the same motifs, but Anna's is different from any other known tapestry, fig. 50.

The composition of the central panel is determined by three friezes with inscriptions, triangular in shape. Below them are rows of small men, shown frontally, and the text shows that they represent the generations of Christ, from Adam to Ram. The uppermost, horizontal inscription reads: GOD FATHER ARD RIS GLØMSDAL ANNA; a little further down we find

IGD and 1760. The figures below this inscription are most likely to represent the Trinity and, on the right, possibly Anna Rasmusdatter and her parents. The clothes are typical of the 18th century, and there seems every reason to assume that Anna is here shown as a bride. She was to have married in 1760, and this may be a bridal tapestry. The initials indicate that the other two tapestries belonged to Anna's older sisters, but they were woven too late to have formed part of their trousseaux, fig. 51. They have three horizontal rows of human figures, with inscriptions above. In the top row we see Joseph, the Virgin with the Child, the three Magi (Balthasar is dark-skinned) and, on the right, the adult Jesus. The two lower rows show the five wise and the five foolish virgins, as well as two men on the far right, whose names are given. It is possible that they stand for Jacob, who was given both Rachel and Leah, and his son Joseph, who came to Egypt and became Lord of the land.

It seems unlikely that these three sisters wove the tapestries themselves. Torø's tapestry has the initials GER in the border, and TRD GSD just below the date 1760. Her sisters' have GSD in the border – this, as well as the just as anonymous GER may stand for the weavers. The name or initials of the artist or craftsman appear not infrequently together with those of the owner, his family or farm, on articles produced in the countryside. – These three tapestries are very fine examples of the weaver's craft. The details of the garments are picked out with metallic thread, and Anna's tapestry has a beautifully made fringe along three sides. Very few Norwegian tapestries can be assigned to a place, milieu and date, and thus these three provide us with valuable evidence about the textile crafts that flourished in Gudbrandsdalen. The 18th century was a rich period for many of the farms here, the people of the valley were open to new impulses, and unusually many craftsmen were at work. Folk art was at its highest peak from the 1760s onwards, but tapestry weaving had lost much of its popularity in most parts of Norway by then.

The wise and the foolish virgins

The most popular subject of Norwegian tapestries is
undoubtedly the parable of the five wise and the five
foolish virgins, who went forth to meet the bridegroom.
When he came at midnight, the wise virgins went to
meet him with their lamps burning, while the foolish
ones went to buy oil for theirs. When they came to the
house of the wedding, the door was shut and they were
not admitted. There are at least 75 tapestries showing
these ten virgins. The moral of this parable was in line
with the ideas of the Reformation, and in Renaissance
art the motif occurs on copper engravings.

Fig. 53. A seller of oil at counter. Detail from a mural in Dale church, Sogn. End of 16th cent⬛

Several versions of this motif seem to have been in use at one and the same time. Because of the shape of the tapestries they are usually shown in two rows above each other, divided by a text stating that five of the virgins were wise and five foolish. We can here let one tapestry represent several, for they were largely woven according to a common design, fig. 52.

At the top we see the wise virgins, their lamps raised high; below, the foolish ones hold their extinguished lamps and cry into their handkerchiefs. They all wear bridal crowns, and their elegant clothes very largely represent the fashions of the first half of the 17th century. The upper part of the bodies is frontal, but they turn slightly from the waist, so that their ornate skirts are seen partly in profile, and they overlap a little. – This must be a faint reflection of the original, which surely employd more movement to express the dramatic situation and the virgins' state of mind. The haloed figure at the top left must be Christ, the bridegroom. The man at the bottom right may be the seller of oil, standing behind his counter. A mural in Dale church in Sogn shows a merchant holding a scale in his hand, fig. 53, and one of the virgin tapestries has a highly moral inscription written on the counter.

One cushion cover manages to find room for the

. 54. Cushion cover
h the wise and the
olish virgins. Natural
ck, beige?, yellow,
ite, red, orange, blue
d green. 17th century.
x 70 cm. Marked RTD.
n, V. Slidre.
rwegian Folk Museum,
lo.

entire motif, with two rows of virgins with their lamps and handkerchiefs, against a background of roofs, towers and battlements. Christ appears to be wearing a cloak, while the seller of oil, who is standing inside his tent, is dressed in the fashionable clothes of a Renaissance courtier, fig. 54. The intials KID are woven in, and the inscription ends ANNO 16... A pity we do not know the exact date, for another cushion, with HLS and the date 1698, fig. 55, has one wise and one foolish virgin, and a comparison would have been of interest.

Fig. 55. Cushion cover two virgins, woven initi HLS and ANO 1698. Natural black, yellow, white, blue and green. x 67 cm. Norwegian Folk Museu Oslo.

Girls in a row

The virgins underwent the same changes as other tapestry motifs, becoming more and more frontal. The different backgrounds which had, in the earliest specimens, been the outline of a town, a landscape with trees or a room with leaded glass windows, were superseded by ornamental patterns against a neutral ground, while the inscription became a narrow ribbon. Not infrequently one or more of the virgins wear the married woman's little dark cap instead of a bridal crown, fig. 56. The two men can no longer be identified. In the end they disappear, or an extra virgin takes their place. The difference between the wise and the foolish virgins was wiped out, and the rows of virgins become rows of crowned girls. In fact we may see these rows of

Fig. 56. Here a married woman with the appropriate black cap stands among the virgi The representation is simplified, and the effe of depth around the figures has disappeare Deep colours. 194 x 12 cm. Museum of Applied Ar Oslo.

76

crowned girls as an independent design, which may have been created in rural Norway.

A tapestry from Orkdal may be indicative of local tapestry production in the 18th century. Here the girls stand in two panels, their feet in opposite directions, fig. 57, and there are eight-petalled roses between their elongated crowns. The severity of these panels is in contrast to the central panel, showing a horseman, a banqueting scene and a musician, surrounded by various filling ornaments, fig. 58. Another tapestry has the girls as a central frieze, while the motif of the wide side panels – a central rosette with four radial twigs of foliage – really belongs to cushion covers, fig. 59.

Some west Norwegian rural tapestries with rows or pairs of girls, fig. 60, were woven with the figures standing, not lying sideways in the loom, which shows

Fig. 58. The musician w an important person on festive occasions. Here the 18th century "portrays" him. Detail f fig. 57.

Fig. 57. Rows of virgins have become rows of g A banqueting scene, a horseman and a musicia At least as typical of a wedding in the countryside of Norway a of the wedding at Cana. Between 1700 and 175(Orkdal, Sør-Trøndelag. The Nordiska Museet, Stockholm.

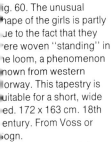

Fig. 59. Wide tapestry, an
unusual format. Three
lengths sewn together.
Central frieze with girls in a
row, side panels with a
pattern resembling a row
of cushion covers. 18th
century, Ogna, Rogaland.
Norwegian Folk Museum,
Oslo.

Fig. 60. The unusual
shape of the girls is partly
due to the fact that they
were woven "standing" in
the loom, a phenomenon
known from western
Norway. This tapestry is
suitable for a short, wide
bed. 172 x 163 cm. 18th
century. From Voss or
Sogn.
Museum of Applied Art,
Oslo.

that tapestry weaving had penetrated into a region dominated by a different technique, with chequered designs. These chequered tapestries were in the west used for the same purpose as our figurative ones, mainly as bedspreads, fig. 61.

Figurative and chequered tapestries are simply two variants of one main technique, and they were traditionally woven on different upright looms. Figurative tapestries have free designs, and where two colours meet in a vertical line, a displaced slit is usually employed, see p. 86. As the name indicates, chequered tapestries consist of square patterns, and the different colours are vertically joined by means of dovetailing, see p. 86.

Fig. 61. Chequered tapestry with lozenge-shaped squares and sma crosses. Yellow, white a natural black on a red ground. Interlocking. 169 134 cm. Norway, district unknown.
Museum of Applied Art, Oslo.

. 62. Tapestry with a
dal couple among
integrated floral motifs.
d, blue, yellow, white
d natural black on a
lish brown ground.
de. 129 x 163 cm.
obably between 1750
d 1800. Lærdal, Sogn
 Fjordane.
rwegian Folk Museum,
lo.

New Times –
New Customs

Even though the first figurative tapestries were woven
in Bergen before 1600, the technique never really
gained a foothold in the west. However, the preserved
textiles show that certain districts, such as Sogn and
Voss, had professional tapestry weavers. A delightful
mid 18th-century tapestry from Lærdal in Sogn has a
bridal couple among a confusion of patterns, fig. 62. As
is typical of the west, there is no dividing line between
the motif panel and the borders – in some cases borders
are lacking altogether. A veritable jungle of vegetal
remains surrounds human figures and animals. This is
really a sign of degeneration – the days of the tapestries
had come to an end. A tapestry with small, obviously

uneasy "virgins" on a monotonous background illustrates another variant of this final phase, which may have extended into the 19th century in western Norway, fig. 63.

We have seen that the early tapestries had naturalistic figures and scenes surrounded by a decorative frame, and we have traced the process leading to stylization and degeneration. We have also noted that the markedly ornamental tendencies of peasant art gave the figures a new kind of context.

Shortly after the last war, Thor B. Kielland recorded about 1250 preserved Norwegian figurative tapestry-woven items, some of them at home, others abroad. Only about 200 of these are large tapestries. It is thus clear that the large figurative tapestries must have been a valuable investment for those who acquired them, in towns or in the countryside. They never became commonplace objects, and it was very rare for one family to own several. They are listed in the accounts of the estates of rich farmers and of public officials, as a symbol of their wealth. Most of them must have formed part of an urban milieu, but because of changing fashions as well as the tooth of time, practically none of these survive in their original setting.

Ancient Norwegians textiles again gained popularity

early in the 1880s and this led to a revival of tapestry weaving, clearly related to similar movements in other countries. In Scania in Sweden tapestry weaving had been practised until fairly recently, but in Norway the technique, and with it the ancient term "Flemish" weaving had died out, and in the middle of the 19th century more general, international terms were taken into use.

During the century that has passed since this revival, a number of scholars have studied their historical background as well as the purely technical problems they present. A great deal has been accomplished, but much remains to be done. Archives and family histories can yield much valuable information, which must then be collated with other local traditions, written as well as oral.

The large figurative tapestries, probably used as bedspreads, are the most important of all the old Norwegian textiles woven in Gobelin technique. Not only were they decorative – they also served to bring learning and morals to people for whom literacy was not a matter of course. The symbolism of the motifs was understood by all, even that of those motifs which appear completely devoid of meaning to later generations.

Modern research is beginning to provide us with the key to this ancient realm of ideas.

g. 64. Cushion cover ith "tulip" motif. Probably ased on a copperplate ngraving from a book oout botany. The tulip is nusually graceful and fills e area with its root, stalk nd flowers. Many colours n a blue ground. The itials IKD occur on everal similar cushion overs. 57 x 56 cm.
1710. Acquired from ovre.
useum of Applied Art, slo.

About Materials and Pigments

Our tapestries were as a rule woven on a warp of linen, wool was used in some very few cases. The earliest professionally woven tapestries also have some linen and metallic thread used for special effects. Silk occurs only in textiles connected with foreign textile traditions. A few 18th-century textiles also include some linen and metallic thread. The wool used varied in quality, but most of it was smooth, strong and lustrous, with long fibres, from the outer coat of the Norwegian short-tailed sheep, the *spelsau*. It was firmly spun and twisted, usually into a two-ply yarn.

Some of the most difficult problems connected with our tapestries concern the colours. The spun yarn was dyed with vegetable dyes, most of them native to Norway. Many of the tapestries are now so faded that they give an entirely incorrect impression of their original colours. Most of our native vegetable dyes are not fast, and the effect of washing, light and air has changed them greatly in the course of the years. The fastness of colours also depends on the preparation of the yarn prior to dyeing, the "mordanting". The colours are often better preserved on the reverse, and sometimes traces of colour remaining within the plying can provide a clue.

Traces of red frequently occur in parts, which have

Fig. 65. These horsemen in jackets, breeches and skull caps are surely related to the three magi, but their clothes are not elegant as those of the magi, who are dressed at the height of Continental fashion. Loose back of chair, 52 x 180 cm. 18th century.
Museum of Applied Art, Oslo.

faded into a pale reddish brown or yellowish white. In such cases the pigment may derive from *Ochrolechia Tartarea* (Mass.), a lichen which produces warm, bright reds with a tinge of blue. This plant, the medieval "purpure of the North", has one drawback – it is not fast to light. To some extent this is true of many of our native pigments, especially the yellows and yellowish greens. Even bright brassy yellow may be reduced to greyish yellow or beige; where yellow and blue had been mixed to produce green, often only the blue remains.

There was an established dyeing tradition long before the days of tapestry weaving, but we know little about early dyeing in Norway, and thus we cannot say whether the tapestry weavers introduced new pigments, new methods. As a general rule the colouring of the urban tapestries was more naturlalistic than the bright, strong colours and contrasts of the later, rural tapestries. But Thor B. Kielland's statement to the effect that 17th-century tapestries were mainly red, blue and yellow, while the 18th century substituted white for some of the yellow, is an over-simplification. These textiles once had a colour spectre so varied and intense that we would find it quite overwhelming today.

No systematic investigation of the materials, colours and techniques employed in all our tapestries has ever been carried out. A few, specially selected pieces have been copied in the course of the last 40 years, in order to elucidate every aspect of the process of tapestry weaving. These detailed studies have provided us with considerable information, with the result that we can now view this heritage in a new light. Else Halling, who led this work in Norsk Billedvev A/S until 1967, states that it is impossible to create anew the original, looking as it did when it came off the loom. What we can do is to arrive at what was typical of the period, at the personal style and colour spectre of each weaver. Many exciting problems are still waiting to be solved by scholars interested in further research on the subject.

Fig. 66. A weeping virgin with her large, fine "handkerchief". Detail from a cushion cover, fig. 64.

About Techniques

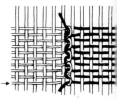

Tapestries woven in the technique once known as Flemish have a weft of threads which interweave with only part of the warp, which they cover entirely. The different colours remain within their own pattern areas. The weft does not pass over the entire width of the fabric.

SINGLE LOCK

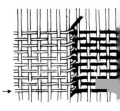

Changes of colour are produced by means of long, narrow wedges woven into the adjacent colour area, hachures. Where the colours meet parallel with the warp, open slits result, and long slits are later sewn up. Cf. the large tapestries from the workshops in the weaving centres of the Continent.

Open slits can be avoided in various ways:

TURNING AROUND ONE END, TOOTHING

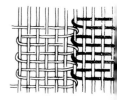

1. The weft threads cross between adjacent ends before returning to their own colour areas. If they cross at *every* meeting we have a "double lock", with a raised ridge at the back of the fabric. If they cross at *every other* meeting, we have a "single lock", with a ridge which is practically unnoticeable.
2. The weft threads are turned alternately around a common end without crossing.
3. The weft threads are turned alternately, in groups, around a common end, toothing.
4. The weft threads are turned around adjacent ends beyond the edge limiting their colour area. In this way the edge is regularly displaced to either side of this limit, and we speak of displaced slits.

DISPLACED SLITS

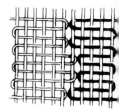

Fig. 67. Loom of the type used for tapestry weaving. Chequered tapestries were woven on this loom within living memory. Tveite, Øvre Hålandsdal, Hordaland. (See: Hoffmann, 1958.)

Bibliography

Bøe, Alf: Tre billedtepper fra Gudbrandsdal. En identifikasjon. Nordenfjeldske Kunstindustrimuseum. Årbok 1959–60. Trondheim 1961. English summary.

Dedekam, Hans: Baldisholteppet. Kra 1918. French summary.

Fischer, Ernst: Hoffet i haven och Salomos visdom. Kunstindustrimuseet i Oslo. Årbok 1972–75. English summary.

Fischer, Ernst: Johanneslegenden inom nordisk flamskväveri. Norveg, Folkelivsgransking 12, 1965. English summary.

Fischer, Ernst: Flamskvävnader i Skåne. Lund, Corona, 1962. German summary.

Fischer, Ernst: Norska flamskvävnader i Nordiska Museet. By og Bygd 18. Oslo 1966. German summary.

Gjesdahl, Karin Mellbye: Vevkunst i Valdres. (Valdres Bygdebok. Bind V, 2. del. Leira 1964).

Halling, Else: Gamle tepper – ny inspirasjon. Kunstindustrimuseet i Oslo. Årbok 1972–1975. English summary.

Hauglid, Roar: Omkring et billedteppe fra Skjåk. Herodesteppet fra 1613. (Foreningen til norske Fortidsminnesmerkers Bevaring. 1961.) English summary.

Hoffmann, Marta: 1800-årenes nye billedvev i Norge og litt om utviklingen senere. Vestlandske Kunstindustrimuseum. Årbok 1963–1968. Bergen 1969. English summary.

Hoffmann, Marta: En gruppe vevstoler på Vestlandet. Noen synspunkter i diskusjon om billedvev i Norge. Oslo, Norsk Folkemuseum, 1958. English summary.

Kielland, Thor B: Norsk billedvev 1550–1800. Oslo 1953–1955. 3 bd. (Fortids kunst i Norges bygder). English summary.

Kunstindustrimuseet i Oslo. Utst. 1946. Norsk billedvev gjennom 400 år. 1540–1940. Fører ved Thor Kielland. [Oslo 1946]. ill.

Nordisk textilteknisk terminologi. Förindustriell vävnadsproduktion. Ny rev. och utökad uppl. utg. av Agnes Gejer og Marta Hoffmann. Oslo, (Tanum), 1974. Swedish, Danish, Icelandic, Norwegian, Finnish, English, French and German terms.